AI For Everyone

A Simple Guide for Older Adults to Understand and Use Artificial Intelligence.

By Chris White

Copyright Page

Title : AI For Everyone: A Simple Guide For Older Adults to Understand and Use Artificial Intelligence.
Author: Chris White
ISBN: 9788409573158
First Edition
Printed in United Kingdom

For permissions or inquiries, contact:
Chris White- yt4tood@yahoo.com

Dedication

For my parents who inspired my thirst for learning

Table of Contents

Preface

Artificial intelligence once felt like something reserved for scientists and tech experts. But as AI quietly becomes part of our daily lives, from smart assistants to online shopping and AI agents, it's clear that this technology is for everyone, no matter your age.

Inspired by my parents and seeing how daunting the concept of AI was to them, I wrote *AI For Everyone* to help older adults understand and feel confident using AI. This book offers simple explanations, relatable examples, and practical tips designed to remove the fear and replace it with curiosity and empowerment.

Whether you're new to technology or just want to stay connected in an evolving world, this guide is here to walk beside you. It's never too late to learn something new.

Chris White

Introduction: Why This Book?

Technology changes fast. Sometimes so fast it feels like the world is moving without us. But it doesn't have to be that way. This book was written with *you* in mind: someone who's curious, practical, and maybe just a little unsure about all the talk of Artificial Intelligence, or AI.

You've likely heard about AI on the news, from your children or grandchildren, or seen it pop up in apps you use. Maybe it feels complicated or intimidating. The good news? You don't need to be a computer expert to understand AI. You just need clear explanations, real-life examples, and a little curiosity.

In this book we'll explore what AI actually is, how it's already part of your life (often without you even realizing it), and how you can benefit from it, safely and confidently. We'll look at well-known tools, like voice assistants and ChatGPT, and lesser known but equally powerful systems that are reshaping healthcare, transportation, and more.

We'll also talk about the limits of AI in terms of what it *can't* do (at least not yet), and why people are concerned about where it's headed.

Whether you want a better understanding of the changing world around you, keep up with conversations, or even try using AI yourself, this book is here to help you every step of the way.

Let's start from the beginning.

The Evolution of Everyday Technology

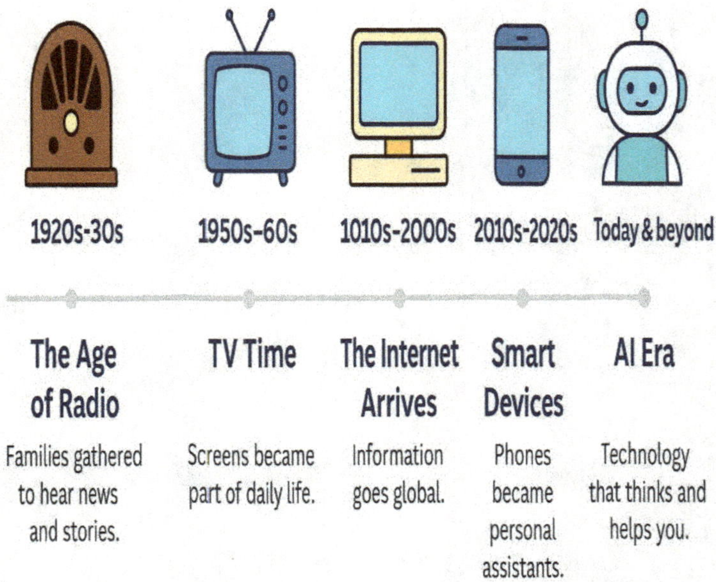

Chapter 1
What is AI?

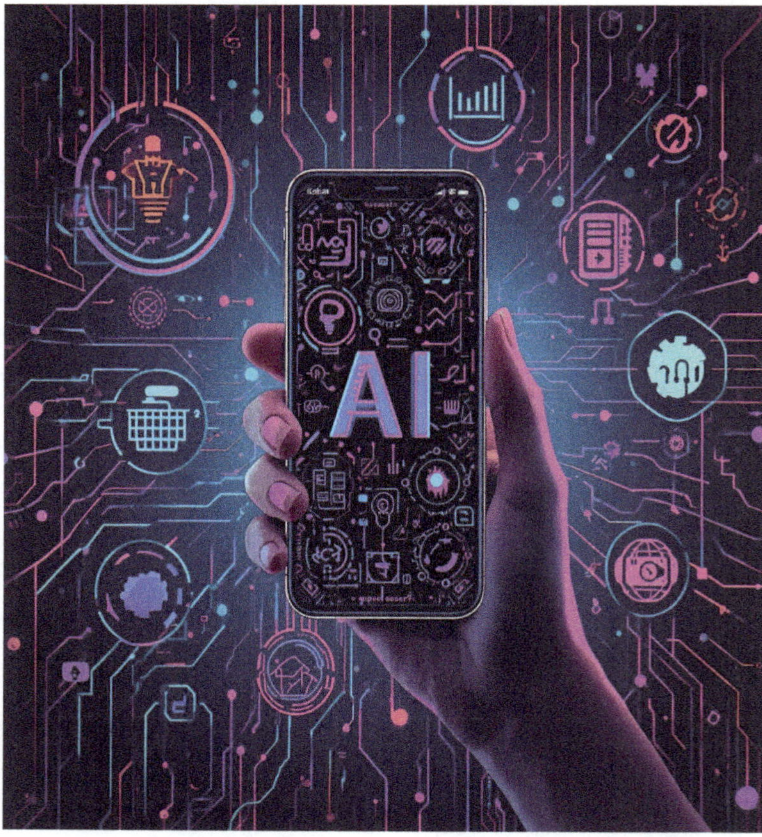

The new technology that is the biggest thing since the internet

A New Tool

We've all seen those science fiction movies. Set in the distant future, a character has a computer personal assistant that performs tasks for them. Remember KITT from the TV series *Knight Rider* or HAL 900 from the movie 2001*: A Space Odyssey?* Just 20 years ago this seemed like pure fantasy. Now we have a form of this type of personal assistant in our homes and on our phones. Think Alexa or Siri. Now imagine having a computerised personal assistant that sends and responds to emails for you, books holidays or does your financial planning for you while you sleep. Thanks to AI, these types of things will all be possible in the very near future.

So, what exactly is AI?

Understanding the Basics

Artificial Intelligence, or **AI** as it is commonly referred to, is when machines like computers, smartphones, or even smart speakers have the ability to "think" or make decisions like a person would. Of course, they don't truly think or feel, but they follow rules and learn from patterns to help us in practical ways.

If you've ever used Google Maps to find your way, spoken to Alexa or Siri, or received movie suggestions on Netflix, you've already interacted with AI.

Everyday Analogy: Your Helpful Assistant

Think of AI like a helpful assistant. You give it instructions, and it tries to carry them out. Sometimes it gets things right, sometimes it needs clarification. But unlike a person, it learns from data, not experience. Also, unlike a person, it has a huge memory and can bring up information or perform tasks such as extensive research in mere seconds. Something that would take a human, months, even years, to do by themselves.

Types of AI

There are different "levels" or kinds of AI:

Narrow AI: This is the kind of AI we have today. It's good at specific tasks, like recommending a movie or identifying a photo of your cat. But it can't do everything, only what it's trained to do. Chatbots like ChatGPT and Claude are this form of AI and are quickly becoming the preferred method when researching information online. Google, the well-known established search engine used by everyone, has developed its own AI version, Google Gemini.

General AI: This is what researchers are still working toward. It would be able to think and reason like a human. Like you may have seen in a science fiction movie. Geoffrey Hinton, the considered "Godfather of AI", believes this will occur in the next four to ten years.

More on that in Chapter 11.

AI in Everyday Life

AI might seem complicated, but it's already working quietly behind the scenes in tools you probably use often:

- Voice assistants like Alexa and Siri
- Spam filters in your email
- Smart thermostats that adjust based on your habits
- Online shopping that suggests items you might like
- Autocorrect and predictive text on your phone

These tools use ***machine learning***, which means they get smarter the more they work with you.

What AI Can and Can't Do

While AI is smart, it's not perfect.

It can:

- Recognize your voice
- Understand simple commands
- Help organize your calendar
- Recommend products or content

But it can't:

- Feel emotions
- Think creatively like a human
- Understand context like people do
- Replace the wisdom and empathy that comes with human experience

AI is a tool, not a replacement for real connection or common sense.

Fun fact

AI can recognise and respond to human emotions through facial and voice recognition.

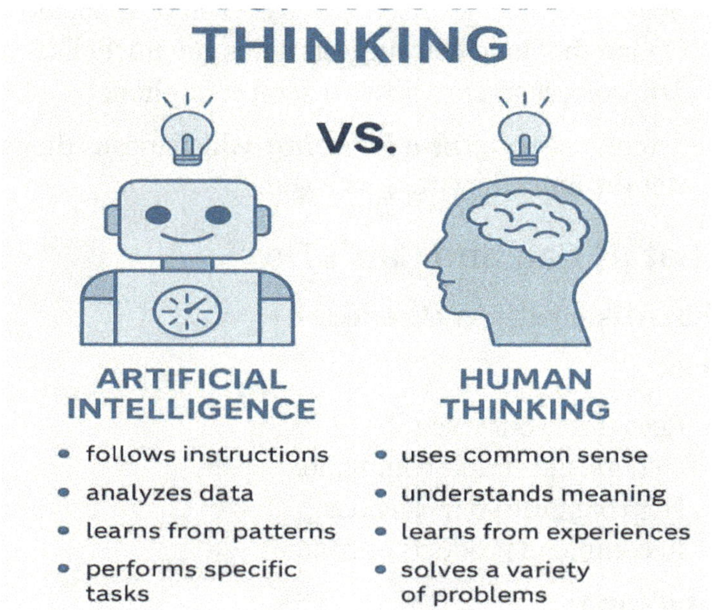

Chapter Summary

- AI helps computers and machines make decisions or predictions
- You already use AI in things like maps, email, and voice assistants

- It learns from data, not from feelings or experiences
- It's here to help, not to take over

Reflection

What kinds of things do you think AI might be able to help you with in your daily life?

Chapter 2
A Short History of AI

From Ancient ideas to everyday tools: How AI went from fantasy to reality

The Origins of a Big Idea

Artificial Intelligence might seem like a modern invention, but the idea has been around for centuries. Early stories and myths from ancient Greece spoke of mechanical men made to serve humans. But it wasn't until the 20th century that real progress began.

In the 1950s, computer scientists like **Alan Turing** began to ask, *"Can machines think?"* Turing even proposed a test (now called the **Turing Test**) to determine if a machine could behave like a human in conversation. This simple idea laid the foundation for modern AI. Turing is famous for inventing the Enigma machine which was used to crack secret German communication codes during World War 11. The world's first programmable computer, named *Colossus,* was constructed during that same period and was designed by telephone engineer Tommy Flowers, based on plans developed by mathematician Max Newman. Some of Turing's previous work contributed to the understanding and design of such machines.

The First AI Programs

By the 1950s and 1960s, the first computer programs were created that could play games like chess or solve math problems. These early systems were basic and needed specific instructions for everything they did.

At the time, many scientists believed we'd have human-level AI within a few decades. But they soon realized that teaching computers to see, hear, or understand language was much harder than expected.

The Rise of Machine Learning

In the 1980s and 1990s, a new approach emerged: instead of giving computers step-by-step instructions, researchers taught them to **learn from data**. This was the beginning of **machine learning**, which allowed AI to improve over time by finding patterns in large amounts of information.

This learning-based approach opened the door to smarter and more adaptable machines and is the method behind many modern AI tools.

Modern AI: A New Era

Fast forward to today, and we now have AI systems that can write music, create pictures, translate languages, diagnose medical conditions, and even drive cars. These systems are often powered by **deep learning**, a type of machine learning that mimics how the human brain works using artificial "neural networks."

AI is no longer just for scientists. It's part of our phones, homes, and everyday services.

Fun Fact

The term "Artificial Intelligence" was first used in 1956 at a summer research workshop at Dartmouth College. That event is considered the official birth of AI as a field of study!

Chapter Summary

- AI has roots in ancient myths and gained traction in the 1950s.
- The Turing Test proposed a way to measure machine intelligence.
- Early AI programs were limited and required detailed instructions.
- Machine learning allowed AI to improve by learning from data.
- Today's AI is everywhere. From voice assistants to self-driving cars.

Reflection

Think back over your lifetime. Can you remember a time when a new technology amazed you? How does AI compare to that experience?

Chapter 3:
How AI Works (No Tech Lingo)

No tech degree needed. Just a little curiosity!

Brains Made of Code

Artificial Intelligence may seem magical, but at its core, it's just a clever way of using **math**, **data**, and **logic** to make decisions. Think of AI as a very fast, very smart calculator that learns as it goes.

Instead of following a fixed set of rules like a traditional computer program, AI looks at **examples** (called data), notices **patterns**, and then makes **predictions** or choices based on what it has learned.

Learning Like a Child. But Faster

Imagine teaching a child how to recognize a dog. You'd show them pictures and say, "This is a dog." After seeing enough examples of different breeds, sizes, and colours, they learn what a dog usually looks like.

AI learns in a similar way. But instead of a child, you're feeding information into a computer program. You might give it thousands (or millions) of pictures labelled "dog" or "not dog." The program studies the patterns in the images and builds a kind of "mental model" to recognize new dogs it hasn't seen before.

This process is called **training,** and the result is a **model** that can make decisions or predictions.

Machine Learning, and Deep Learning. What's the Difference?

You might hear other terms thrown around, like "machine learning" or "deep learning." Here's what they mean:

Machine Learning: A way for computers to learn from data without being told exactly what to do. For example, a spam filter can learn which emails are junk based on examples it's seen before. It can learn what your movie preferences are and give recommendations. Voice assistants like Siri or Alexa learn your voice patterns and preferences and can do things like set reminders.

Deep Learning: A more advanced type of machine learning that uses layers of "neural networks" or computer systems inspired by the human brain. While regular machine learning might need help to learn things and figure stuff out, deep learning can comprehend complex tasks on its own. This is the step towards AI becoming more autonomous. Some deep learning examples are facial recognition technologies, self-driving cars and medical diagnosis.

You don't need to remember all the technical stuff. Just know this: AI is the big idea.

Machine learning is one way to make AI work.

Deep learning is a more advanced, autonomous and complex version of machine learning.

What AI Needs to Learn

To train an AI system, three things are essential:

1. **Data** – Lots of examples (text, images, sounds, etc.).
2. **Algorithms** – Instructions that help AI learn patterns.
3. **Feedback** – Correct answers that help it learn from mistakes.

Over time, the AI becomes better at its task, whether it's recognizing a face, understanding speech, or suggesting a movie.

Different Types of AI Learning

There are a few main types of learning AI uses:

- **Supervised Learning**: Like a student being taught with answer sheets.
- **Unsupervised Learning**: The AI looks at data without labels and finds patterns on its own.
- **Reinforcement Learning**: Like training a dog with treats, it's rewarding the AI when it gets something right.

What is an Algorithm?

An **algorithm** is just a set of rules the computer follows to solve a problem. Think of it like a recipe. If you follow the steps, you get a result. Like baking a cake.

In AI, algorithms help the computer sort through data, recognize patterns, and make choices based on what it has learned.

For example:

- If you like crime genres, mysteries and documentaries, Netflix's algorithm might recommend a new crime series.
- If your phone hears the words "Call John," an algorithm helps it figure out who "John" is and how to reach him.

Algorithms are everywhere online. Ever noticed how you start seeing more of certain types of products or topics while you are searching online or checking social media? That's an algorithm learning about you from your searches and online habits and then tailoring everything to suit your preferences. This can be a good thing and a bad thing. It can make finding the things you like and want more of, much easier. However, it limits what you see and experience, filtering out the things it believes you may not want to see or be interested in.

What is a Model?

Once AI has been trained, the set of rules and knowledge it creates becomes a **model**. You can think of it like a trained musician. Before learning to play the instrument, they studied notes, rhythm, and scales. After a lot of practice, they can now play songs smoothly. The trained musician is like an AI model, ready to perform based on everything it has learned.

Different models do different jobs:

- One model might predict the weather.
- Another might suggest what groceries to buy.
- A large language model like ChatGPT or Claude can write, summarize, and answer questions using natural language.

Garbage In, Garbage Out

AI is only as smart as the data it learns from. If the data is messy, unfair, limited or imprecise, the results will be too. This is why it's important for AI to be trained carefully and why it sometimes makes mistakes.

For example:

- If a facial recognition system is only trained on photos of young people, it may not work well on older adults.
- If an AI is fed news from unreliable sources, it might spread misinformation.

That's why human oversight is still very important and necessary.

AI Doesn't "Think" Like A Human

Even though it might *look* like AI is thinking, it's not. AI doesn't have feelings, understanding, or awareness. It doesn't know *why* something is true. It only knows patterns it has learned. It is after all, a machine.

When ChatGPT writes a poem or your voice assistant tells you the weather, they're not conscious. They're repeating or mimicking patterns from learned data, not forming original thoughts. At least for now.

Putting It All Together

Here's a simple version of how AI works:

1. **Data Collection**: The AI is given lots of examples (text, images, sounds, etc.).

2. **Training**: The AI looks for patterns and learns from them.
3. **Model Building**: It forms a system to apply what it's learned.
4. **Prediction or Response**: You ask it something, and it gives you an answer based on its training.
5. **Feedback** (sometimes): If the answer is wrong, people correct it, so the AI improves over time.

Not Magic. Just Math.

AI may *feel* like it can think or feel, but it doesn't understand like we do. It doesn't feel joy, worry, or intent. It's doing what it's been trained to do: spot patterns and respond.

You Don't Have to Know Everything

You don't need to remember every term or process to use AI. Just like driving a car, you don't need to understand the engine to go for a ride. But having a basic idea of what's happening gives you more control and more confidence.

In the following chapter, we'll explore how AI shows up in everyday life. You might be surprised how often you're already using it.

Fun Fact

Your smartphone's autocorrect and voice assistant (like Siri or Alexa) use AI that was trained on millions of words. Yet they still sometimes make hilarious mistakes!

Chapter Summary

- AI learns by spotting patterns in data.
- It mimics learning by using examples, much like we do.
- It needs data, instructions (algorithms), and feedback to improve.
- There are three different learning types that AI uses: supervised, unsupervised, and reinforcement.
- AI isn't magic. It's simply advanced math and pattern recognition.

Reflection

Have you ever taught someone a skill by showing them examples like knitting, baking, or fixing something? That's a bit like how AI learns. Can you think of a task you do regularly that AI might be able to learn?

Chapter 4
Everyday Examples of AI

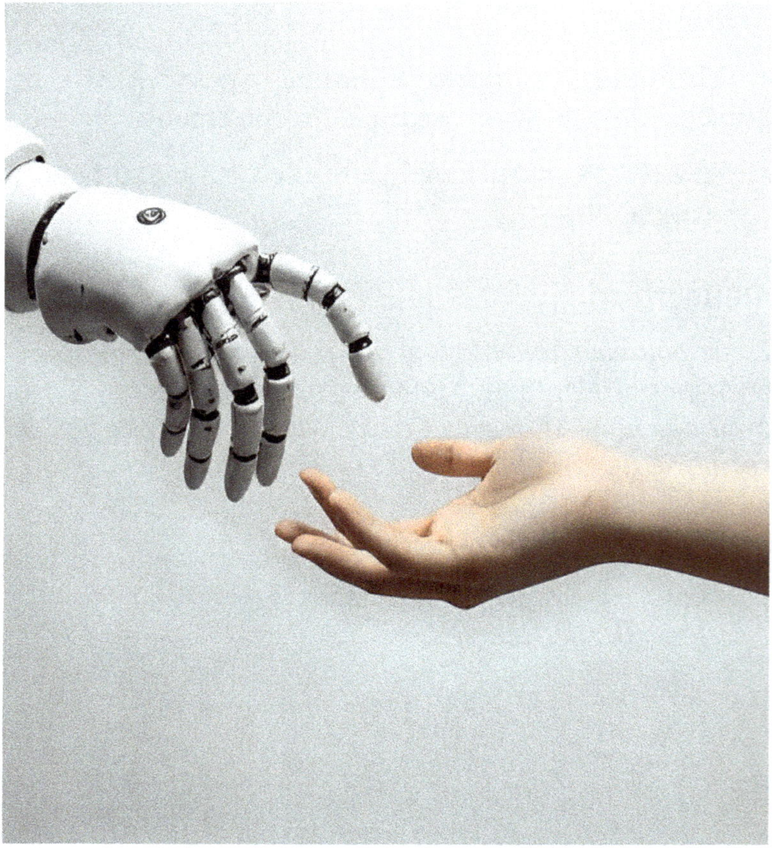

You're probably using AI more than you think!

AI in Your Pocket

Take a quick look at your smartphone. If you've used voice assistants like **Siri**, **Alexa**, or **Google Assistant**, you've used AI. These helpers can answer questions, set reminders, and even tell jokes, all by understanding and responding to your voice.

Even simpler features like **predictive text** (guessing what word you'll type next) or **autocorrect** rely on AI. They're trained on thousands of common word patterns to help you type faster and with fewer errors.

AI in Your Living Room

Ever watched a movie one time on **Netflix**, **YouTube**, or **Amazon Prime** and noticed how they recommend shows or films? The more you watch a specific type of movie the more those types and genres of movies appear in your recommendations feed. That's AI too! These systems learn your preferences by watching what you click, watch, or pause. Then they suggest content you might like. Like Tom Hanks movies? Netflix's AI will recommend them to you. A great way to discover films you didn't know about.

The same thing happens with **Spotify**, **Apple Music**, or even **online news** apps. They tailor what they show you using AI that learns from your habits. Spotify has an AI assistant called *The DJ* that creates playlists and suggests new songs to listen to based on your previous listening choices.

AI Around the House

AI can also power smart home devices:

- **Smart thermostats** learn your room temperature preferences and adapt to the season.
- **Smart doorbells** (like Ring) detect motion and can recognize familiar faces.
- **Robot vacuums** map your floors and clean without you lifting a finger.

Even your **digital photo album** may use AI to sort photos by people's faces, places, or events.

AI in Your Health and Safety

Healthcare is becoming smarter too:

- **Wearable devices** like smartwatches track your heart rate, steps, and sleep.
- Some apps can detect **irregular heart rhythms** or remind you to move or drink water.
- Hospitals use AI to **analyse medical images**, predict health risks, and even assist doctors in diagnosing conditions.

In emergencies, AI-powered **fall detection** systems can alert family or emergency services when needed.

AI in Photos and Facial Recognition

Your phone or tablet might organize your photos using facial recognition, grouping pictures of people together even if you didn't label them. That's AI recognizing faces, even as people age or change hairstyles.

Apps can also help enhance blurry images, remove red-eye, or even suggest the best photo out of a group.

AI in Retail and Shopping

Beyond online shopping suggestions, AI is changing how stores manage inventory, stock shelves, and even price items.

- **Personalized coupons** based on your previous shopping habits and preferences.
- **Self-checkout machines** that recognize items faster
- **Smart shelves** that know when to reorder products

Some grocery stores like *Amazon Go* use AI cameras and weight sensors to let you walk out with your items and get charged automatically. No cashier needed. You simply scan your credit card or a QR code on an app when you enter, and then AI through the cameras and shelve sensors, works out which items you have selected and then charges your credit card.

But **beware**...If you decide you don't want an item, make sure you put it back exactly where you got it from otherwise you will still be charged!

If you search on YouTube, you will find videos of Amazon Go in action.

AI in Banking and Security

AI helps spot fraud by watching for unusual spending on your accounts. If you've ever received a call or message about a suspicious charge, that alert likely came from an AI system.

Banks also use chatbots to answer basic questions or help reset passwords.

AI in Transportation

You don't need a self-driving car to benefit from AI in travel. Transportation systems are becoming smarter and safer thanks to intelligent systems.

- **Real-time tracking** of buses and trains
- **Safer cars** that brake or stay in lanes automatically
- **Flight operations** that predict and reduce delays

Modern cars can now "see" a vehicle in your blind spot and warn you before you switch lanes. That's AI using sensors to keep you safe.

AI in Emergency Services

First responders and emergency systems are using AI to save lives and speed up response times.

How it helps:

- **Predicting where accidents may occur**
- **Dispatching ambulances** faster based on traffic data
- **Analysing 911 calls** to prioritize serious cases

Some cities use AI to detect gunshots instantly and send help to the exact location, faster than a person might be able to call for help.

Behind the Scenes

AI also works quietly in the background when you:

- **Shop online** (helping suggest items)
- **Use GPS** apps like Google Maps (predicting traffic)
- **Call customer service** (some chatbots are AI-based)
- **Search the internet** (search engines use AI to rank results)

You don't always see it, but it's there. Helping things run more smoothly.

You're Already Living with AI

As you can see, AI isn't science fiction. It's now very much a part of everyday life. And you've probably been using it for years without realizing it.

The more you know about where it shows up, the more confident you can be in using it to your advantage.

Fun Fact

AI helped a man in Canada identify a rare heart condition after his smartwatch noticed an unusual rhythm. The device sent an alert, and doctors confirmed it could have saved his life!

Chapter Summary

- AI is already a big part of daily life: phones, TVs, homes, and health devices use it.
- AI through learning about you and your preferences, can suggest entertainment, control home environments, and track your health.
- Many features we rely on (like search, directions, and online shopping) are powered by AI.
- Most of the time, we use AI without even realizing it.

Reflection

What AI-powered tools do you already use without thinking about it? Are there any new ones you'd like to try, like a voice assistant or health tracker?

Chapter 5
Meet ChatGPT

Your AI conversation partner. Friendly, helpful, and always ready to chat.

Say Hello to ChatGPT

ChatGPT is a **chatbot**. A computer program designed to have conversations with people. But unlike earlier chatbots that followed simple scripts, ChatGPT uses powerful AI to understand your questions and respond in a surprisingly human way.

You can ask it to explain things, tell a story, write a poem, or help you with a task and it will generate a thoughtful answer in seconds. There are other AI chatbots like Claude, Google Gemini, Microsoft Copilot and Perplexity AI. But it's ChatGPT that is the most talked about and well known. For this reason, we will look specifically at ChatGPT, but the other chatbots perform similar functions.

How Does It Work?

ChatGPT was trained using **a massive amount of text** from books, websites, and articles. This gave it a general understanding of how people communicate. It doesn't "think" or "know" in the way humans do, but it can **predict words and sentences** that make sense based on what you ask.

ChatGPT can now browse the internet in real time. But it mainly gives answers based on what it has learned during training. So, it's best used for general information, creative help, or conversational support. Crucially it is learning all the time and adapting to your wants and needs. The more you use it, the better and quicker the results.

Where Can You Use It?

You can access ChatGPT on:

- A web browser (at openai.com/chat or apps that use it)
- Some smartphones and smart devices
- Integrated apps like Microsoft Word, Bing, or certain voice assistants

ChatGPT also has its own app that you can download from Play store on your Android phone and Windows PC or the Apple store if you have an iPhone or Mac.

What Can ChatGPT Do?

ChatGPT can do all sorts of things.

- **Answer questions**: Ask about things like history, science, hobbies, almost anything. Even AI!
- **Write content**: Emails, birthday cards, stories, even recipes.
- **Translate text**: Convert languages like French to English with reasonable accuracy. At the moment the best translation AI app is considered to be DEEPL
- **Help brainstorm**: Things like gift ideas, travel plans, conversation starters.
- **Practice conversation**: Great for language learners or just chatting.
- **Explaining Difficult Concepts Simply**: "*What is cryptocurrency?*" or "*How does a pacemaker work?*"
- **Writing Help**: Draft letters, emails, poems, or birthday messages.
- **Learning and Memory Aids**: Summarize books, create study guides, or help remember names and dates.

- **Entertainment**: Write short stories or suggest movies.
- **Planning**: Help organize travel plans, daily schedules, or meal ideas.

Fun Ways Older Adults Use ChatGPT

There are many fun and interesting ways you can use ChatGPT. From sourcing information to entertainment. It really is all down to you.

- **Write poems** or letters to grandchildren
- **Find new hobbies** or learn about history
- **Get** book or movie **recommendations**
- **Ask** for **jokes** or **quotes** to brighten your day
- **Practice writing** or even try creative **storytelling**

What Are ChatGPT's Limitations?

As amazing as it seems, ChatGPT isn't perfect.

- **It doesn't "know"** in the human sense. It predicts what to say based on patterns and data it has learned, not personal understanding or common sense.
- **It may sound confident but be wrong.** Always double-check important facts (like medical or financial advice).

Privacy and Safety Tips

When using ChatGPT it can sometimes seem you are talking to another human, particularly if you are not used to using AI. Its friendly tone may make you feel comfortable enough to share personal information and data. ChatGPT doesn't store personal conversations or access your devices, but it's still important to be careful:

- Don't share passwords, banking details, or private health information.
- Use it to *support* your decisions, not *replace* your doctor, lawyer, or financial planner

Fun Fact

*The "GPT" in ChatGPT stands for **Generative Pre-trained Transformer**. But don't worry. You don't need to remember that. It just means it was trained to "generate" language like we do.*

Chapter Summary

- ChatGPT is a powerful, friendly AI chatbot.
- It uses language prediction to answer questions and chat naturally.
- You can use it to write, brainstorm, learn, or even be creative.
- It's not perfect, but it's a helpful tool when used wisely.

Reflection

What would you ask ChatGPT if you could try it right now? A question you've always wondered about? A letter you need to write?

Chapter 6
Creating with Canva

A Friendly Tool for Visual Creativity

Unlocking Your Creativity

Have you ever wanted to make a birthday card, flyer, photo collage, or even a digital book cover, but felt overwhelmed by the software available? Enter **Canva**. An online design platform that makes creativity simple, fun, and surprisingly powerful.

Canva allows anyone, even those with little to no design experience, to create beautiful visual content. It's used around the world by professionals and beginners alike. But don't let the word "design" intimidate you. Canva was built to be user-friendly, and it's especially perfect for older adults who want to explore visual storytelling, hobbies, or small business projects.

What Is Canva?

Canva is a free, web-based design tool (also available as an app) that lets you create and customize visuals like:

- Greeting cards
- Posters and flyers
- Social media posts
- Photo albums
- Presentations
- Book covers (like this one!)
- Resumes and newsletters

It offers pre-designed **templates** which are ready-made layouts. All you need to do is drag and drop your content (like text or pictures) into place. Many of these templates have been created by designers and are quite impressive. You can choose different fonts, colours, and even animated effects. There are many different types of templates for creating eBooks, business reports, newsletters, wedding invitations, Videos, just to name a few.

Canva has large data base of photos, graphics, artwork, logos charts and other useful imagery you can add to your design. It also has an app called *Magic Media* which allows you to create an image by giving simple prompts.

For specific creations, particularly when using Magic Media, Canva works on a token system in which you are offered a specific number of tokens to "Pay" for your creations. This is quite common for many AI apps. However, in the free version, most of the things you can create don't require you to spend tokens.

How Does Canva Use AI?

Believe it or not, Canva uses **AI-powered tools** to make the design process easier:

- **Magic Resize**: Automatically resizes your design to fit different platforms like Facebook, Instagram, or email.
- **Text Suggestions**: AI can suggest headlines and captions.
- **A Background Remover**: Can instantly remove backgrounds from photos and other images with one click. You can then add your own background using other images or colours. Whatever takes your fancy.
- **Design Assistant**: Offers smart suggestions to make your design look balanced and visually appealing.

These features work quietly in the background to help make your designs look professional. No graphic design degree needed!

Why Older Adults Love Canva

- **It's easy to use** with a simple drag-and-drop system.
- **It's inspiring**, sparking creativity and giving you new ways to express yourself.
- **It's useful**, whether you're printing a family recipe card or helping a community group with flyers.
- **It's social**, allowing you to share creations with loved ones, online or in print.
- **It's empowering**, giving you full control of the creative process.

Fun Fact

Over 100 ***million people*** *around the world use Canva—many of them over the age of 50! It's one of the most popular design tools online and is available in over 100 languages.*

Chapter Summary

Canva is a design tool that allows you to create beautiful visual projects with ease. Thanks to its intuitive interface and AI-powered features, even beginners can make professional-quality designs. Whether for fun, family, or function, Canva offers a wonderful way to express yourself creatively.

Reflection

Have you ever tried creating something visual, like a card or a poster? How did it go?
What might you like to create using Canva?
Perhaps a family recipe book or holiday card?

How do you feel about trying out a new creative tool, especially one designed to be simple and friendly?

Chapter 7
Prompts: Talking to AI Made Simple

Speaking in AI isn't complicated. It's just knowing what to say and how to say it!

What Is a Prompt?

A **prompt** is the message or question you give to an AI system like **ChatGPT**. It's how you "talk" to the AI to ask it to do something.

Think of it like typing a question into Google, but instead of getting a list of websites, **the AI gives you a direct answer**.

Examples of prompts:

- "Tell me a joke about cats."
- "Help me write a thank-you letter to my granddaughter."
- "Explain the difference between weather and climate."
- "Give me 5 healthy dinner recipes for one person."

Why Prompts Are Important

AI chatbot tools don't work on their own. They respond to **your input**. The better your prompt, the more helpful and accurate the AI's response will be. Think of AI as a person who speaks your language as a second language. It may understand what you ask, but it doesn't comprehend the nuances or subtexts. It thinks literally. If you are not clear and precise in what you ask AI, it may give you a completely wrong response.

A good prompt:

- Gives the AI **clear direction**
- Helps the AI **understand your tone or style**
- Can include details like length, audience, or purpose

How to Write a Good Prompt

Start simple! Then, if needed, add a bit more detail.

Basic Prompt	Improved Prompt
"Write a poem."	"Write a short, funny poem about turning 70."
"Help me cook dinner."	"Give me a healthy recipe for chicken I can prepare in 30 minutes."
"Tell me about history."	"Explain World War II simply for someone who didn't study history."

Adding details and being specific is important. Things like your goal, audience, tone (friendly, formal, etc.), or format (list, story, paragraph) can lead to better results.

Prompting Tips for Older Adults

- **Be specific**: *"Explain this like I'm a beginner"* or *"Use simple language"* really helps.
- **Try different styles**: *"Write it as a poem"* or *"Make it sound cheerful."*
- **Ask follow-ups**: After the first answer, you can ask, *"Can you explain that more?"* or *"Can you make it shorter?"*

And remember...**you can't break it!** AI won't get annoyed or offended. Play around and see what it can do.

Fun Prompt Ideas to Try

- *"What are some fun things to do in [your city] this weekend?"*
- *"Write a birthday message for a friend who loves gardening."*
- *"Explain what cryptocurrency is in simple terms."*
- *"Plan a week of easy meals for two people."*

Chapter Summary

- A **prompt** is what you type to tell the AI what you want.
- The clearer and more detailed your prompt, the better the answer.

- Prompts can ask for writing, facts, recipes, summaries, jokes, and more.
- You can always **revise** or **follow up** to improve the result.

Reflection

What is something you'd like help with this week? An email, a recipe, a fun activity? Try turning it into a prompt and give it a try.

Chapter 8
What Are AI Agents?

Smart helpers that can take action on your behalf.

Meet Your Digital Helpers

Imagine having a helpful assistant who doesn't just answer your questions but also takes action for you. That's what AI agents are all about.

AI agents are like digital helpers that use artificial intelligence to make decisions and do tasks for you automatically. While a chatbot like ChatGPT answers questions, an AI agent might book an appointment, send an email, or even order groceries all by itself, based on your preferences. Currently AI agents are being developed for just about anything as technology advances and developers discover what is possible.

What Makes It an 'Agent'?

An AI agent is a little different from a regular AI assistant. Here's why:

- It has a goal: Like scheduling your doctor's appointment or finding the best travel deal.
- It makes decisions: Based on what it knows, it picks the best path to reach the goal.
- **It takes action:** It can interact with websites, devices, or software, not just talk to you.

Think of it like this: If a regular AI is a smart dictionary, an AI agent is a personal assistant that reads, writes, and acts for you. This makes the rise of AI agents very significant as they are proactive, while ChatGPT in its current form, is a largely passive tool.

Examples of AI Agents

There are currently thousands of different AI agents and many more are being created every day. As technology grows so do their capabilities. Here are some examples and what they can do.

Replika: AI Companion Agent

- **What it does**: Acts as a personal companion you can chat with. It remembers your conversations and tries to offer support and meaningful dialogue.
- **Use**: Emotional support, practicing conversations, or simply chatting when feeling lonely.
- **Why it's helpful**: Great for people who want friendly interaction or someone to talk to at any time.

xAI's Grok Agent (Elon Musk's AI)

- **What it does**: Connects with your X (formerly Twitter) account to respond to messages, search posts, and summarize content.
- **Use**: Social media help, keeping up with trending topics, or automating online activity.
- **Why it's helpful**: Saves time and reduces effort on platforms that can be overwhelming.

Google Assistant Routines

- **What it does**: Controls lights, thermostats, music, and reminders based on your voice or schedule.
- **Use**: *"At 7 PM, turn off the lights, lock the door, and play soft music."*

- **Why it's helpful**: Makes your home smarter and safer without lifting a finger.

Microsoft 365 Copilot

- **What it does**: Works within Microsoft Word, Excel, and Outlook to write, edit, summarize emails, and create presentations.
- **Use**: *"Write a professional email," or "Summarize these 50 emails."*
- **Why it's helpful**: Helps older adults stay productive and organized without needing tech skills.

Clara or x.ai (AI Scheduling Agents)

- **What they do**: Manage your calendar by scheduling meetings via email.
- **Use**: You copy them in on an email, and they act like a personal assistant coordinating dates/times with others.
- **Why it's helpful**: No back-and-forth emailing. Your AI agent handles it for you.

Auto-GPT / BabyAGI

- **What they do**: These agents can set their own goals, break them into steps, and work toward completing them using online tools or apps.
- **Use**: *"Research vacation options. Use preferences to create an itinerary."*
- **Why it's helpful**: They do complex, multi-step tasks with little input.

- *Note: These are more experimental and not always stable for general use yet.*

Instacart AI Shopping Assistant

- **What it does**: Suggests grocery lists based on your diet, past purchases, or recipe needs.
- **Use**: *"Create a list for a week of meals for a diabetic diet."*
- **Why it's helpful**: Takes the stress out of planning and shopping. Great for dietary needs.

DoNotPay: AI Legal Agent

- **What it does**: Helps you contest parking tickets, cancel subscriptions, or request refunds using AI-generated legal arguments.
- **Use**: *"Write a complaint letter about a wrong charge."*
- **Why it's helpful**: Saves a lot of time, money, and stress. especially for those who dislike paperwork.

Key Features Many AI Agents Share:

- Work in the **background** once set up
- Learn and **improve over time**
- Communicate using **natural language (like talking or typing)**
- Designed to help you **save time, reduce stress, and make decisions**

The Future of AI Agents

AI agents are becoming more powerful every year. Soon, you may have a single agent that:

- Knows your calendar and health needs
- Helps with errands or reminders
- Understands your style of communication
- Learns and improves over time

They're not perfect, and they still need guidance. But they're built to make life easier. Very useful if you find technology overwhelming or tiring to manage.

Fun Fact

Some companies are testing AI agents that can manage your finances, including paying bills and recommending better insurance or savings plans.

Chapter Summary

- AI agents go beyond just chat. They take actions on your behalf.
- They're used for travel, scheduling, home automation, email, and more.
- They follow goals, make decisions, and learn from your preferences.
- These tools are still growing but may soon help with many everyday tasks.

Reflection

If you had a digital helper that could take care of one task for you each week, what would it be?

Chapter 9
The Benefits of AI for Older Adults

From reminders to relationships. How AI can lend a helping hand.

Everyday Support

AI can take some of the stress out of everyday life. Need a medication reminder? Want to control your lights with your voice? Curious about the weather? AI tools like smart assistants can help you do these things hands-free.

Health and Wellness

Wearables and health apps powered by AI can:

- Track steps, sleep, and heart rate
- Alert you to irregular patterns
- Help manage conditions like diabetes or high blood pressure

Some apps even connect with doctors or caregivers, creating a safety net that wasn't possible before. If you fall or hurt yourself, there are AI apps that alert emergency services and family members.

Connection and Companionship

AI can also help people feel **less isolated**. Video calling assistants, translation tools, or even friendly chatbots offer ways to stay connected. Ideal if mobility or travel is a challenge.

Learning and Growth

You can use AI to learn something new: a language, a hobby, or a skill. AI tutors and learning apps are available 24/7 and adapt to your pace.

Fun Fact

Some retirement homes now use robot pets powered by AI to provide comfort to residents with memory challenges. No pet hair and no litter box required!

Chapter Summary

- AI can help with task reminders, health tracking, and communication.
- It offers tools to stay connected and feel supported.
- It can enrich life with learning, entertainment, and safety.
- The goal isn't to replace people, but to **assist and empower** you.

Reflection

Which AI feature would make your daily life easier or more enjoyable? Something for your health, home, or just for fun?

Chapter 10
Staying Safe with AI and Technology

Smart tools are great. But smart habits are even better.

Privacy Matters

AI tools often collect data to work better. That's helpful, but it's important to know:

- What information you're sharing
- Who you're sharing it with
- How to manage privacy settings

Always review the privacy settings on apps and devices when connected to the internet. It is important that you ensure that you are limiting the possibility of sharing of private information inadvertently. Before you sign up to anything or start using an app, read all the privacy and security settings carefully.

Avoiding Scams

AI has made some scams more convincing. Fake phone calls or emails that sound real. Be cautious when:

- Someone asks for money or personal information
- An offer seems too good to be true
- You're contacted by someone you don't know

When in doubt, ask a trusted friend or family member to help review it. AI has the ability to mimic your voice. So always check with somebody face to face or with trusted others before sending money online or believing what you hear on the phone.

Deep Fake videos and photos are images created by AI to look real. As though the subject of the video is doing something that in reality they are not. You may have seen

Deep Fake videos of politicians or celebrities on TV or online. At the moment these videos are very obvious, the depictions of the people too polished and cartoonish. But they are getting better. So, check personally with someone before believing what you see online.

Google Veo 3 can now produce very realistic photos and videos from a simple prompt. While *Higgsfield AI can* create realistic videos and images of you in any setting you like.

Recognizing AI Limits

AI isn't always right. It may:

- Make up facts
- Misunderstand what you ask
- Give outdated information
- Misspell or misplace a word or give totally different information to what you asked it. This can happen if you use ChatGPT in busy periods

It is important to always double-check anything important, especially medical, legal, or financial info. While in general the information ChatGPT and other chatbots provide you is accurate, it is only as precise as what is has learned or interpreted from what you asked it. This is why how you write prompts is so important. Always good to check the information before presenting it as fact or correct.

There have been examples of businessmen who decided to copy and paste what ChatGPT told them into presentations only to discover during the presentation the information was incorrect.

AI Can Be Biased

AI learns from the data it's given. If that data includes stereotypes or unfair patterns, the AI may repeat them, even if it doesn't mean to.

Example: If past job hiring data unfairly favoured one group of people, an AI trained on that data might make the same mistake.

That's why **humans must always supervise and test AI systems**, especially in important areas like hiring, healthcare, or the legal system.

AI Is Only a Tool. Not a Decision Maker

It's tempting to rely on AI to make decisions for us. But that can be risky.

- A doctor might use AI to read an X-ray but still needs to make the final call.
- A teacher might use AI to generate lesson ideas but still tailors them for students.
- You might use AI to plan your meals, but you know your health and taste better than any app.

Humans must remain in charge. AI is here to help and act as an assistant. Not to lead.

AI and Human Emotions

AI can **simulate** emotions. It can write a love letter or a poem. But it doesn't feel what it writes. And while it can create art, music, and stories, it lacks the **personal life experiences** that inspire real human creativity.

Fun Fact

There are AI companions programmed to provide emotional support, show empathy and ask personal questions through text, voice notes and pictures. Some humans have even claimed to have fallen in love with their AI companion!

Chapter Summary

- Be aware of what you share and where.
- Look out for scams, especially ones using AI voices or fake messages.
- AI isn't perfect. Always verify important info.
- Good habits + smart tools = safer use of technology.

Reflection

Have you ever encountered a suspicious phone call, email, or message? What would help you feel more confident using new technology safely?

Chapter 11:
The Future of AI

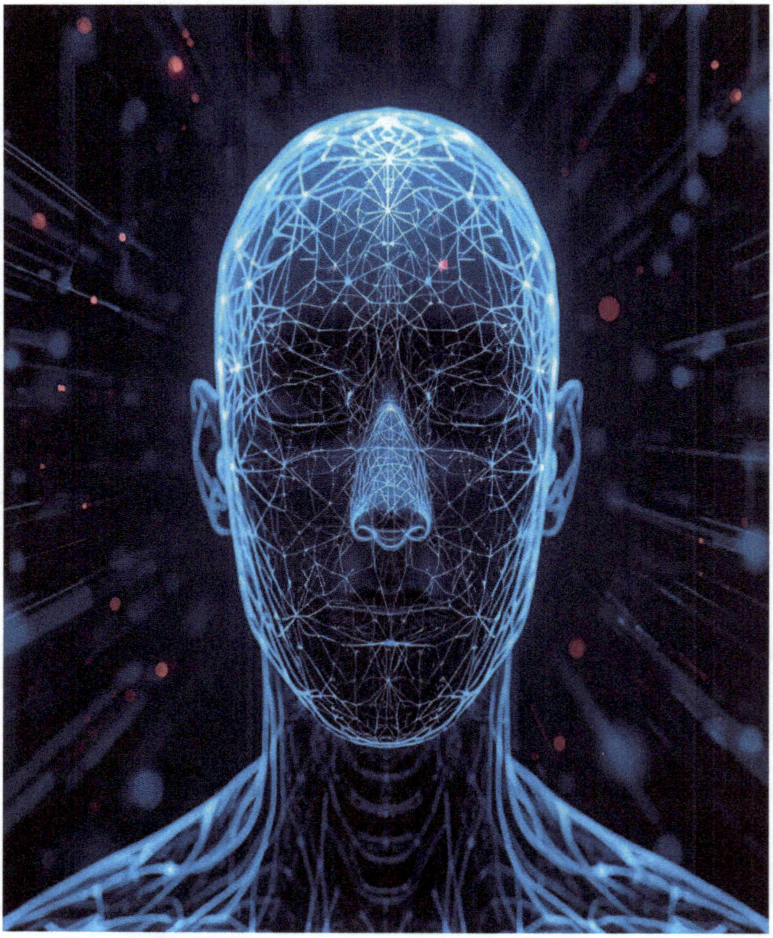

What's next for AI and what it could mean for you.

The Road Ahead

AI is advancing quickly. It's moving from performing specific tasks to **learning broader skills**. For example, some systems can now:

- Summarize complex documents
- Compose original music or art
- Simulate voices and video

But we're not at science fiction-level intelligence. Not **yet**.

AI and Society

Everyday Life with Smarter AI

As AI becomes more advanced, it will blend even more into daily life. You may see:

- **Smarter homes** that adjust lighting, heating, and security automatically
- **Personal AI assistants** that manage your calendar, order groceries, and remind you of appointments
- **Health monitors** that detect problems before you feel symptoms
- **Robots that help around the house**, especially for older adults who want to stay independent

Example: Imagine an AI that reminds you to drink water, take your medicine, and even calls for help if you fall.

AI in Work and Business

In the future, it is likely AI will take over more routine or dangerous jobs. But it will also create new kinds of work.

- **Repetitive tasks** like data entry, scheduling, or assembly line work may be automated
- **Creative and human-focused roles** like caregiving, teaching, and arts will still rely on people
- **New jobs** will emerge that we can't imagine yet. For example, nobody predicted careers like app developers or social media managers 30 years ago

Lifelong learning may become the norm, even for older adults. AI could be your teacher, career coach, or project partner.

AI in Healthcare and Longevity

Healthcare may be one of the biggest beneficiaries of AI:

- **Virtual doctors** that diagnose minor issues at home
- **Personalized medicine** based on your genetics and lifestyle

- **AI companions** that support mental and emotional well-being
- **Advanced prosthetics and brain-computer connections** to restore mobility or communication

For older adults, AI could offer **more years of independence, safety, and companionship**.

Education and Relationships

AI could support education across all ages:

- **Customized learning**: AI tutors that teach based on how *you* learn best
- **Language learning**: Speak to your AI in Spanish, French, or any language you want to pick up
- **Family connection**: AI tools that help you write stories, share memories, or create videos to pass down to your grandchildren

It might even help people stay connected across generations and cultures.

Concerns About the Future

Alongside the excitement, many people feel nervous—and understandably so. Common concerns include:

- **Privacy**: Who controls your personal data?
- **Job loss**: What happens if automation replaces too many roles?
- **Bias and fairness**: Will AI treat everyone equally?

- **Control**: How do we prevent misuse or overreliance on AI?

These concerns are being taken seriously by researchers, leaders, and communities. Many believe the solution lies in **responsible development, ethical design, and public involvement**, including older adults like you.

What Is AGI?

Artificial General Intelligence (AGI) is a term for an AI that could learn and think like a human across many different areas. Think KITT from Knight Rider. It's still theoretical, but researchers are working toward it.

AGI would be able to reason, plan, and even understand context. Things that currently AI still struggles with. This would give it independent thought and the ability to act on its own accord.

Why Do People Want AGI?

Scientists and engineers are excited about AGI because it could:

- **Solve complex problems** like climate change or disease cures
- **Work across many fields** not just one task
- **Help in areas where skilled workers are limited**
- **Support aging populations** with caregiving and companionship

Imagine an AGI that could be your personal doctor, teacher, financial planner, and even friend, learning your needs and adapting over time.

Are We Close to AGI?

No one knows exactly **when** AGI will be developed. Experts disagree on how soon it might happen:

- **Some say**: Within 10–20 years. Some much sooner.
- **Others believe**: It could take much longer or might never happen at all

While today's AI seems smart, it's still missing key parts of true intelligence:

- Understanding cause and effect
- Learning from experience in the real world
- Making wise, ethical decisions

AGI Brings Big Questions

Creating something as intelligent as a human raises *serious* questions:

- **Safety**: How do we ensure AGI doesn't cause harm, either accidentally or on purpose? How do we know that all it has learned and been trained on is good for humanity?
- **Control**: Who gets to decide how AGI is used and who benefits? Controlling a powerful AGI gives a country huge advantages over its rivals and enemies.
- **Ethics**: Should an AGI have rights under the law? Could it have emotions? Feelings?
- **Jobs**: What happens if AGI can do most work better and cheaper than people?

That's why governments, scientists, and ethicists are already working hard to build rules and guidelines *before* AGI arrives.

Will AGI Replace Us?

This is one of the biggest fears people have.

But most experts and scientists believe the best future is one where **humans and AGI work together**, not compete. Like any powerful tool, AGI could be used for great good or great harm, depending on *how* we choose to use it.

The key is making sure AGI reflects our values, protects human rights, and supports, not replaces, our lives and communities.

What Can You Do?

You don't have to be a tech expert to stay informed and prepared:

- **Ask questions**: Don't be afraid to explore and learn.
- **Stay curious**: Try AI tools in small ways. Ask ChatGPT a question, test a voice assistant, or try a health app.
- **Join the conversation**: Talk with younger people, attend a workshop, or read more. Your perspective matters.
- **Advocate for your values**: Speak up about fairness, safety, and dignity in AI tools that affect your life.

A New Chapter for Everyone

AI will change many parts of life. But one thing won't change:

The importance of human wisdom, experience, and connection.

You've lived through great changes before: TV, the internet, smartphones. And you've adapted and thrived. AI is just the next chapter, and your insight is as important as ever.

Final Thoughts

You don't need to be afraid of AI. It's okay to be cautious. Learn about it. Use it wisely. Stay involved.

AI is not just for the young or the tech-savvy. It's a tool for *everyone*, including you.

Whether you're using it to stay in touch with family, manage your health, explore new interests, or simply satisfy your curiosity, AI has the potential to enrich your life.

The future is not just about machines. It's about people and how we use these tools to build a better world.

Fun Fact

In 2023, GPT-4 passed the Uniform Bar Exam exceeding the average human score, scoring in the 90th percentile.

Chapter Summary

- AI is becoming more capable, creative, and widespread.
- **AGI** is the idea of a machine that can think and learn like a person.
- It doesn't exist yet, but many are working toward it.
- AGI brings hope for big breakthroughs. But also, big responsibility.
- The goal is to make AGI safe, fair, and helpful for all.
- AGI could one day think more like a person.
- AI will affect jobs, laws, and the way we live.

- Staying informed is the best way to prepare for the future.

Reflection

How do you feel about the future of AI? What excites you and what worries you?

Conclusion
Getting Started with AI

Take the first step. Your future self will thank you.

Starting Your AI Journey

Explore at your own pace. The more familiar AI becomes, the less intimidating it feels. Explore different chatbots and AI agents to see what works best for you. Most of them offer a free option and a more premium option where you have to pay for their use, but in general the free options are good and easy to use.

And remember. You're never too old to learn something new. AI can be a partner on your journey, offering support, curiosity, and connection.

You've come a long way in this book. From understanding what AI is, to meeting ChatGPT, to looking ahead at the future of Artificial Intelligence. Whether you're excited, cautious, or simply curious, one thing is clear:

AI is no longer just science fiction. It's here and it can be a helpful part of everyday life.

And the best part? It's never too late to learn or try something new.

5 Simple Steps to Get Started with AI

Here are a few easy ways to dip your toes into the world of AI. No experience required:

1. Try ChatGPT

Start with something familiar and friendly like ChatGPT.

- Visit chat.openai.com on your computer, tablet, or phone. There is also an app you can download.

- Sign up with an email (or ask a friend to help)
- Type a question like:

"What's an easy recipe with chicken and rice?"

"Tell me a fun fact about the 1960s."

"Write a birthday message for my grandson."

You'll see how easy and conversational it is.

2. Use a Voice Assistant

If you have a smartphone or smart speaker, try using:

- **Siri** (Apple devices)
- **Google Assistant** (Android or Google devices)
- **Alexa** (Amazon devices)

Ask it:

"What's the weather today?"

"Remind me to take my medicine at 8 PM."

"Play some relaxing music."

These are everyday AI tools designed to help you.

3. Explore with a Family Member

If you're unsure about trying it alone, ask a grandchild, friend, or neighbour to show you:

- How they use AI to study, work, or organize
- How to install and use apps that involve AI (like health trackers or photo organizers)

It can be a great way to learn *together*.

4. Use AI for a Hobby

Do you enjoy:

- **Gardening?** Ask AI for seasonal tips.
- **History?** Ask about past events or famous figures.
- **Writing?** Try co-writing a poem or story with ChatGPT.
- **Puzzles or games?** Ask it to create a trivia quiz or riddle.

Start with what *you* enjoy.

5. Keep Learning at Your Own Pace

You don't have to master it all at once. Here are gentle ways to keep learning:

- Watch simple YouTube videos about AI for beginners.
- Join a tech group or class at a local library or community centre.

- Read articles or listen to podcasts designed for older adults.

You might be surprised how much fun you have along the way.

You Belong in the Future

AI isn't just for young people, companies, or tech experts. It's for everyone. Including you.

Your life experiences give you a unique and valuable perspective on things. Whether you use AI to simplify your day, stay in touch, learn information, develop new skills, or just satisfy your curiosity, you are part of the conversation.

So go ahead. Ask that question. Try that app. Talk to that chatbot.

The future is here. And you're ready for it.

Thank you for reading.

If you enjoyed this book, please leave a review where you purchased it from and help me create more content like this.

May your journey with AI be one of learning, empowerment, and connection.

Appendix: Additional Resources and Glossary

This section provides extra resources and definitions to help you continue exploring AI and expand your knowledge. Whether you're looking for more tools, deeper reading, or just a quick explanation, you'll find useful information here.

Additional Resources

1. Websites and Online Tools for Exploring AI

- **ChatGPT**: Try it at chat.openai.com. Start a conversation with ChatGPT, ask questions, and see how it works.
- **Google Assistant**: If you have an Android phone, Google Assistant can help you with day-to-day tasks. Start by saying "Hey Google" followed by a question.
- **Siri**: For Apple users, Siri can answer questions, send texts, set reminders, and much more. Just say "Hey Siri."
- **Alexa**: Amazon's Alexa can assist with home automation, setting reminders, and playing music. Look for Alexa-enabled devices like the Echo.
- **Coursera**: A site that offers courses on AI and other tech topics, often for free. Check out Coursera.org.
- **YouTube**: Search for "AI for beginners" or "How AI works" to find easy-to-understand videos. Channels like "CrashCourse" and "TechQuickie" provide accessible explanations.

2. Books to Read

- *"Artificial Intelligence: A Guide for Thinking Humans"* by Melanie MitchellThis book provides a clear, balanced look at the current state of AI and its future possibilities.
- *"AI Superpowers: China, Silicon Valley, and the New World Order"* by Kai-Fu LeeExplore how AI is shaping the global economy, with a focus on China and the U.S.
- *"Life 3.0: Being Human in the Age of Artificial Intelligence"* by Max Tegmark. This book looks at how AI will impact life on Earth and explores big questions about the future.

3. AI News and Articles

- **MIT Technology Review – AI Section**: www.technologyreview.com Stay updated on the latest developments in AI and technology.
- **Wired – AI**: www.wired.com/category/aiProvides in-depth stories and opinions on AI's impact on society.
- **AI News**: www.artificialintelligence-news.comA great resource for all things AI-related—from innovations to ethical concerns.

4. Local Classes and Workshops

Many community centres, libraries, and senior organizations offer classes on technology, including AI. Check with your local:

- **Library**: They often host free workshops on tech topics.

- **Community Centres**: Look for local tech groups or meet-ups.
- **Senior Programs**: Some senior organizations offer tech assistance to help you get comfortable with new technologies.

Glossary of Common AI Terms

Here's a list of important terms related to AI, explained simply:

- **AI (Artificial Intelligence)**: Machines or software designed to perform tasks that typically require human intelligence, such as understanding language, recognizing images, or making decisions.
- **Chatbot**: A computer program designed to simulate conversation with human users, especially over the internet. ChatGPT is an example of a chatbot.
- **Narrow AI**: AI systems designed to perform a specific task (e.g., voice assistants, AI for driving cars). They are *narrow* because they only focus on one thing, unlike humans who can multitask.
- **AGI (Artificial General Intelligence)**: A type of AI that can learn and perform any intellectual task that a human can do. AGI is still a future goal, not yet achieved.
- **Machine Learning**: A method of teaching computers to recognize patterns in data, so they can make decisions or predictions without being explicitly programmed to do so.
- **Neural Network**: A type of machine learning modelled after the human brain that can help computers recognize patterns, like identifying faces in photos.
- **Deep Learning**: A type of machine learning that uses large neural networks to analyse big sets of

data. It's often used for more complex tasks like speech recognition or self-driving cars.

- **Natural Language Processing (NLP)**: The ability of a computer to understand and generate human language, like how ChatGPT can understand and respond to your questions.
- **Automation**: The use of technology to perform tasks without human intervention. In AI, this often means machines or software handling repetitive tasks (e.g., automated emails, robotic cleaning).
- **Bias**: When an AI system makes unfair or inaccurate decisions based on biased data. For example, if an AI was trained mostly on data from one group of people, it might not perform as well for other groups.
- **Ethics**: The study of moral questions about how AI should be developed and used. Should AI be able to make life-and-death decisions, for example? Ethical concerns are key in AI development.
- **Algorithm**: A set of rules or steps that an AI follows to perform a task. Algorithms can be simple or very complex, depending on the problem.

Author Bio

Chris White is a passionate advocate for lifelong learning and digital inclusion. With a background in education and many years of experience helping people navigate new subject areas and technologies, Chris is dedicated to making complex topics, like artificial intelligence, accessible and empowering for everyone, especially older adults. As a lifelong learner himself, Chris understands the difficulties associated with learning new skills, particularly as a mature age adult. When not writing or teaching, Chris enjoys challenging himself to acquire new skills and learn new things including reading about emerging tech and exploring how innovation can improve everyday life. *AI For Everyone* is his effort to help bridge the gap between people and the technology shaping our world.